A WIFE'S LITTLE RED BOOK

A WIFE'S LITTLE RED BOOK

Common Sense, Wit and Wisdom for a Better Marriage

Robert J. Ackerman, Ph.D.

Health Communications, Inc.
Deerfield Beach, Florida

www.hci-online.com

©1998 Robert J. Ackerman
ISBN 1-55874-553-X hardcover
ISBN 1-55874-552-1 trade paper

All rights reserved. Printed in the United States of America. No part
of this publication may be reproduced, stored in a retrieval system
or transmitted in any form or by any means, electronic, mechanical,
photocopying, recording or otherwise without the written permission of the publisher.

Publisher: Health Communications, Inc.
        3201 S.W. 15th Street
        Deerfield Beach, Florida 33442-8190

Cover design by Andrea Perrine Brower
Cover photograph by Gerhard Heidersberger
Ring design by Diana Ring Co.
Rings courtesy of Beverly's Jewelers, Ft. Lauderdale, Florida

To
Madeline T. Ackerman
who for more than fifty years
was my father's anchor,
conscience and best friend
and, in return, he loved her.

Introduction

*T*his little book is not intended to tell you how to be a wife. After interviewing more than 500 men, I am attempting to answer the question, "What do husbands want from and appreciate about their wives?"

Hopefully, this little book will give you some insights into the mystery of husbands (trust me, we're not that complicated), bring a smile to your face and provide some helpful hints that keep us happy.

Great marriages are full of ordinary deeds that, as a marriage grows, take on more and more significance. The small gestures that partners do for each other make them feel appreciated and needed, and *that* is what husbands want. Enjoy each other.

When he's driving, let him pretend that he's not lost.

*Let him enjoy
the last two minutes
of the game without
interruption.*

*Leave him
at least a small
space in the shower
to keep some of
his things.*

Don't talk about old boyfriends in front of him.

*When you enter
a party with him
—hold on to
his arm.*

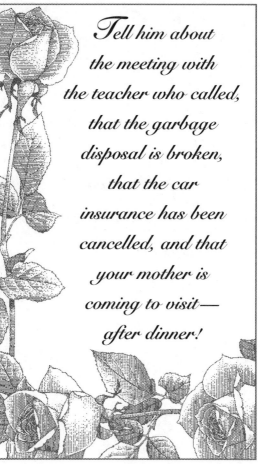

Tell him about the meeting with the teacher who called, that the garbage disposal is broken, that the car insurance has been cancelled, and that your mother is coming to visit— after dinner!

6

*Make time
for him.*

*Let him find out,
by your actions,
not your words,
that he can count
on you.*

8

When he asks,
"What's wrong?"
don't say, "Nothing,"
if there is a problem
and then expect
him to guess
what it is.

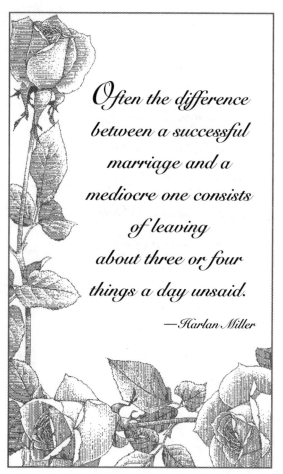

Often the difference between a successful marriage and a mediocre one consists of leaving about three or four things a day unsaid.

—Harlan Miller

Use yesterday's paper, not today's, to wrap something.

*Offer him a
few suggestions,
but not too many.*

*Unless he
asks for help,
leave him alone
when he is fixing
something.*

*Let him brag
about you.*

*He may not
always express himself
clearly or even tactfully,
but remember,
in his eyes you're
beautiful.*

Buy him new underwear. Otherwise, he'll wear the ones he has until they fall off.

Fill a stocking
for him at Christmas
or map out a Valentine's
Day treasure hunt
where the surprise
is —you.
He still likes
surprises.

*American
women expect to find
in their husbands
a perfection that
English women only
hope to find
in their butlers.*

—W. Somerset Maugham

When you are out with him at a restaurant, don't say that you are not hungry, and then eat most of his food.

*When you want
him to volunteer,
ask him first.
Don't volunteer his
time without his
permission.*

On a cold morning, scrape the ice off his car windshield.

Let him keep those same old raggedy pants that he wears every Saturday.

Keep his favorite candy hidden from the children.

*Don't tell him
everything that's in the
newspaper before
he reads it.*

Learn to play or enjoy a sport with him.

Ask him if
there is anything that
he needs when you
go to the store.

*Nothing flatters
a man as much as the
happiness of his wife;
he is always proud
of himself as the
source of it.*

—*Samuel Johnson*

Record checks
that you've written
in the checkbook.

Send him a card at work just to say hello.

*Never open
his mail.*

*Don't remind
him that he is losing
his hair.*

No matter how short the trip, go away with him without the children at least once a year.

*Whatever
he keeps in his
"junk drawer," don't
worry about it.
Just be glad that
it's not all over
the house.*

*Spend a lot of
time together doing
activities you love to
share and less energy
arguing about how
you are different.*

Surprise
him with two
tickets to his favorite
sporting event.

Don't take over his side of the bed when he gets up in the middle of the night to go the bathroom!

Don't over-analyze your marriage. That's like yanking up a fragile indoor plant every twenty minutes to see how its roots are growing.

—Unknown

No matter how much you are tempted, let him discover on his own that the reason the lawnmower won't start is because he forgot to turn the "on" switch.

Appreciate
the small things that
he does for you,
but don't take the
big things for
granted.

*Let him dream.
A man's dreams can
inspire him for
a lifetime.*

Help him
protect his knees;
after you drive his car,
return the driver's
seat to where
he had it.

Keep your
"Honey do"
list short.

*Don't threaten
the children with,
"Wait until your
father gets home!"*

*Flirt with him
once in awhile.*

*Sing and dance
together and be joyous,
but let each of you
be alone, even as
the strings of
a lute are alone
though they quiver with
the same music.*

—Kahlil Gibran

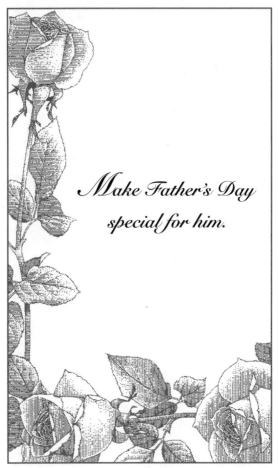

*Make Father's Day
special for him.*

When you

encounter your friends,

help him remember

their names.

Get his car washed.

When you are wondering what he does with all those tools, remember, he may be wondering what you do with all that makeup.

Don't leave a wedding reception or a party without asking him to slow dance with you.

Remember that sometimes when he's quiet he doesn't even know why—he's just being quiet.

Once in awhile
jump all over him
—in bed!

No one likes
being taken for granted.
On his next pay day,
remind him how far
he has come in earning
a living.

Sometimes I wonder if men and women really suit each other. Perhaps they should live next door and just visit now and then.

—Katharine Hepburn

*Offer to
help him shovel
the snow off the
driveway.*

Respect his privacy; don't go through his wallet.

Tape his favorite TV show when he works late.

A good back massage goes a long way.

Take an occasional shower together.

Make an appointment for him for his annual physical exam.

*If you use
his tools, put them
back where you
found them.*

*Don't throw
out his favorite old
shirt with the
holes in it.*

Lots of people want to ride with you in the limo, but what you want is someone who will take the bus with you when the limo breaks down.

—Oprah Winfrey

*Find a compromise
when you disagree
on parenting
techniques.*

Teach your children to respect their father.

Invite his friends
for dinner.

Don't use his "pet" name in front of the guys.

Why does a woman work ten years to change a man's habits, and then complain that he's not the man she married?

—Barbra Streisand

Let him have the

last slice of

pizza.

Wait until halftime of the game to ask him to run to the store.

*When talking
with him on the phone,
ignore call-
waiting.*

*The most
important minutes
of the day are when
you first wake up
and when you first
see each other
after work.*

When he has
played so hard that
even his eyelids hurt,
don't tell him that
he's getting too old;
just draw him
a hot bath.

There are kisses,
and then there are
<u>kisses</u>.
Make sure that
he gets both.

*If possible,
travel with him
on a business trip.*

*When you go
to the movies, get up
and buy the popcorn
and drinks on
occasion.*

A simple enough pleasure, surely, to have breakfast alone with one's husband, but how seldom married people in the midst of life achieve it.

—Anne Morrow Lindbergh

*Ask his advice
when you have
a problem.*

*Buy him a
tape or a CD of
his favorite
music.*

*Try to get
along with his
family.*

Teach him how to sew on a button.

*Give him a
sweatshirt from his
alma mater.*

*Admit when you
are wrong.*

When he tells a story, don't finish it for him.

Take the ultimate challenge— match his socks.

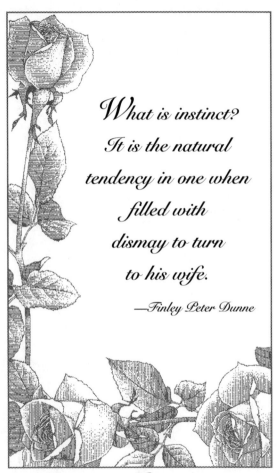

*What is instinct?
It is the natural
tendency in one when
filled with
dismay to turn
to his wife.*

—Finley Peter Dunne

Photograph him with the children.

*Don't talk to him
like his mother
does.*

*Let him know
that you want to be
alone with him.*

*Take his car
in for a scheduled
oil change.*

Put the morning newspaper at his place at the breakfast table.

*Let him spoil
the children once
in awhile.*

*Never tell his
secrets to anyone;
they are for your
ears only.*

Never
starch his underwear
(unless, of course,
you're mad at him).

Married couples who love each other tell each other a thousand things without talking.

—Chinese proverb

*Tell him every day
that you love
him.*

Listen carefully when he talks about his old friends; those guys mean a lot to him, and he is sharing with you a part of his past that he treasures.

*Help him to
learn what you like.
He wants to know
what makes you
happy.*

When you talk about him, lift him up; don't put him down.

Throw only kisses
at him.

Great lingerie

leads to great . . .

Buy him an umbrella and keep it where he can find it.

*If everyone is
having fun, go ahead
and let him roughhouse
with the kids. It may
be his way of
hugging.*

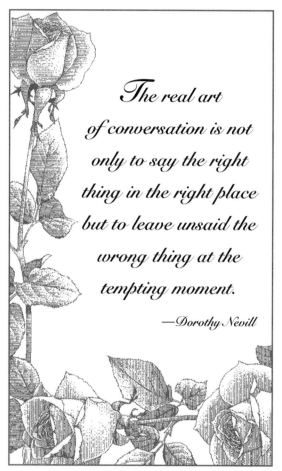

The real art of conversation is not only to say the right thing in the right place but to leave unsaid the wrong thing at the tempting moment.

—Dorothy Nevill

Remember,
"window shopping"
is confusing and not
important to many men.
We just don't
"get it."

*Ask him to
be involved in family
activities with the
children. The years go
by too quickly.*

*Give him a
subscription to his
favorite magazine
and renew it
annually.*

*Give him a
family picture
for his office.*

Teach your husband all about taking care of the baby or the children so that he will be comfortable when he is alone with them.

"You're not going to wear that are you?" is a demeaning question. Let him wear whatever he wants on vacation.

*Buy him an
exercise machine and
encourage him
to use it.*

*I'd rather
have roses on my
table than diamonds
on my neck.*

—Emma Goldman

Wear his favorite perfume.

If he smokes

cigarettes,

encourage him to stop.

Buy him a discount coupon booklet for the local golf courses.

Keep a scrapbook of his career mementos.

Write down his messages.

*Help him
decorate the house
for the holidays.*

*Ask him to carve
the Thanksgiving
turkey.*

*At the beginning
of the season, give
him a dozen new
golf balls.*

Archie doesn't know
how to worry without
getting upset.

—*Edith Bunker*

*Take good
care of yourself—
physically,
emotionally,
spiritually.*

If you don't like his friends, tell him why.

Don't tell him

the ending of the book

or the movie.

*When he is talking,
let him finish without
interrupting.*

Let him use the computer, too.

Be patient at his high school reunion —and remember, they only happen once a decade.

*Never get rid
of his favorite things,
no matter how old
they are.*

*Keep his picture
on the refrigerator door
along with everyone
else's.*

*You never
know till you try to
reach them how
accessible men are; but
you must approach
each man by
the right door.*

—Henry Ward Beecher

Don't let him take all of the pictures on vacation or at special events. Make sure that he is in some of the pictures, too.

When he fixes something around the house, take time to acknowledge his work.

*Throw him a
surprise birthday
party.*

Pay attention
when he is going
over the details of your
family will or estate
planning.
He needs to know
that you understand
what to do and
what you have
planned together.

Sign him up for access to the Internet.

Buy a fire extinguisher for the kitchen and the garage.

Develop an outdoor activity for each season that you both can do together.

Get him an autographed picture or souvenir of his favorite athlete.

*Go for a
walk in the woods
together.*

One kind word can warm three winter months.

—*Japanese saying*

*Give him a
gift certificate to his
favorite store.*

Buy him something that he has always wanted, but wouldn't buy for himself.

*Stock up on duct tape,
plenty of duct tape.
Why? Because it's
a "guy thing."*

Listen to his fears,
but don't tell him
he's afraid.

Give him an address book with all the names, addresses and telephone numbers of the people who are important to him.

*Have an extra
set of car and house
keys made and
put them in a
safe place.*

*Sometimes he needs
to be a big kid; take
him to the amusement
park with the children.*

*Buy him a
new watchband to
replace the one that is
barely held together
with a safety pin.*

*A friend hears
the song in my heart and
sings it to me when my
memory fails.*

—*Pioneer Girls Leader's Handbook*

Stick up for your husband whether he is present or not.

Get a lock
for your bedroom
door.

*Don't spray
paint the lawn
furniture
next to his car.*

Remember him in your prayers.

Have a good pillow fight once in awhile.

*Buy him
a baseball card
of one of his favorite
boyhood players.*

Turn out the lights when you are not using them.

Pick up his prescription for him when he is sick and keep track of when he needs to take it.

*A wedding
anniversary is the
celebration of love, trust,
partnership, tolerance
and tenacity.
The order varies for
any given year.*

—Paul Sweeney

*Buy him
an automobile club
membership for
emergencies.*

Help keep good financial records to make filing your income tax returns easier.

*Encourage him to
have a hobby.*

*When he has
a deadline for a big
job, help him by
completing other tasks
he needs to do.*

*Remind him
when his favorite TV
show is coming on.*

*Make a
video of him when
he is playing
a sport.*

*Sometimes,
without knowing why,
trust his judgment.*

Learn how to drive a stick shift.

One advantage of marriage is that, when you fall out of love with him or he falls out of love with you, it keeps you together until you fall in again.

—Judith Viorst

Learn CPR.

*Don't buy him
cheap tools.*

Pay your bills

on time.

Sometimes you and your husband will look at things differently.

You say, "Guess how much money I saved today?" and he says, "How much did you spend?"

Laugh a lot together. It will get you through many tough times.

Successful
marriages are built
on small things.
Do something every
day to improve your
marriage.

If he wants to sit quietly, don't force him to talk, but let him know that you are ready to listen when he needs you.

Marriage 101

Today's lesson

is priorities:

Husband, children, job.

Husband, children, job.

Husband, children, job.

Any questions?

In the coldest February, as in every other month in every other year, the best thing to hold onto in the world is each other.

—Linda Ellerbee

Husband's Highlights

His Name: _____

Work Address: _____

_____

Work Phone: _____

Birthday: _____

Mother's Birthday: _____

Father's Birthday: _____

Wedding Anniversary: _____

Anniversary of First Date: _____

Favorite Restaurant: _____

Favorite Sport/Activity: _____

Favorite Team: _____

Favorite TV Show: _____

Favorite Store: _____

Favorite Vacation Spot:_____

Favorite Meal: _____

Coat Size: _____ Shirt Size: _____

Shoe Size: _____ Pants Size: _____

Sweater Size: _____ Underwear Size:_____

Other Books by Robert J. Ackerman

A Husband's Little Black Book

Before It's Too Late

Silent Sons

Perfect Daughters

Too Old to Cry

Children of Alcoholics

Growing in the Shadow

Let Go and Grow

Same House Different Homes

Recovery Resource Guide

About the Author

Robert J. Ackerman, Ph.D., is the husband of Kimberly Roth Ackerman, the father of three children and professor of sociology and Director of the Mid-Atlantic Addiction Training Institute at Indiana University of Pennsylvania. He tries to keep his life in that order.

New from the *Chicken Soup for the Soul*® Series

Chicken Soup for the Teenage Soul

Teens welcome *Chicken Soup for the Teenage Soul* like a good friend: one who understands their feelings, is there for them when needed and cheers them up when things are looking down. A wonderful gift for your teenage son, daughter, grandchild, student, friend... #4630—$12.95

Chicken Soup for the Woman's Soul

The #1 *New York Times* bestseller guaranteed to inspire women with wisdom and insights that are uniquely feminine and always from the heart. #4150—$12.95

Chicken Soup for the Christian Soul

Chicken Soup for the Christian Soul is an inspiring reminder that we are never alone or without hope, no matter how challenging or difficult our life may seem. In God we find hope, healing, comfort and love. #5017—$12.95

Chicken Soup for the Soul® Series

Each one of these inspiring *New York Times* bestsellers brings you exceptional stories, tales and verses guaranteed to lift your spirits, soothe your soul and warm your heart! A perfect gift for anyone you love, including yourself!

A 4th Course of Chicken Soup for the Soul, #4592—$12.95
A 3rd Serving of Chicken Soup for the Soul, #3790—$12.95
A 2nd Helping of Chicken Soup for the Soul, #3316—$12.95

Selected books are also available in hardcover, large print, audiocassette and compact disc.

Available in bookstores everywhere or call **1-800-441-5569** for Visa or MasterCard orders. Prices do not include shipping and handling. Your response code is **WLRB**.